Acclaim for LORENZO HERRERA Y LOZANO's

Amorcito Maricón

Whether you like rancheras or oldies or both – throw on your favorite rolas and retire for the night with *Amorcito Maricón*. Lorenzo Herrera y Lozano's poems will enrapture you and remind you that there is pleasure in dolor y amor and that the desire to be loved is at the core of who we are. This collection gets to the heart of what it means to live amid and in spite of our contradictions. *Amorcito Maricón* is for both the hopeless romantic and the militant revolutionary, because at the end of the book you realize that being brown and queer means being both.

Francisco J. Galarte, Ph.D., Assistant Professor of Gender & Women's Studies, University of Arizona

There is something undeniably tender, rasping and raw about *Amorcito Maricón*. Written to the melody of the sweetest bolero and the sounds of the most tragic melodrama, Herrera y Lozano's words are the flesh of desire and love's sorrows, flesh that writes bodies of faith and longing anew. Sung to their own tune, these lyrics enunciate liberation in its most intimate of brown renditions.

Armando García, Ph.D., Assistant Professor of Hispanic Languages and Literatures, University of Pittsburgh

Maricón. Maricón. *Amorcito Maricón*. Gorgeous. Passionate. Powerful. Poetry filled with queer love. Bien good sex. Joto love. Herrera y Lozano is a chingón poet. Ay, maricón, mi maricón. Que lindo eres. Like homemade chile relleno, *Amorcito Maricón* is picoso, sabroso, bien Chicano and a muy Mexicano-caballero love story. Love, love, love streams like agua santa through his poemas. Herrera y Lozano envelopes the beauty, intensity, sensuality, and power of a Chicano gay man. An exquisite craftsman, he sculpts words del barrio y amor.

Verónica Reyes, author of *Chopper! Chopper! Poetry from Bordered Lives*

Amorcito Maricón

POEMS BY
LORENZO HERRERA Y LOZANO
FOREWORD BY ERNESTO JAVIER MARTÍNEZ, PH.D.

*Amorcito
Maricón*

Kórima Press

Credits:
"Hierbaloca: The Children of Aztlán" first appeared in ZYZZYVA: the journal of West Coast writers and artists, Volume 26, #2, Fall 2010.
"On This Lake" first appeared in Yellow Medicine Review: A Journal of Indigenous Literature, Art, and Thought -- International Queer Indigenous Voices Issue, Fall 2010.
"You Bring Out the Joto In Me" first appeared in Tragic Bitches: An Experiment in Queer Xicana & Xicano Performance Poetry (Kórima Press, 2011).
"Chimera" and "Children of Wilted Suns" first appeared in Queer in Aztlan: Chicano Male Recollections of Consciousness and Coming Out (Cognella Academic Publishing, 2013).
Excerpts from "Jotos," "Children of Wilted Suns," "Chicharrón of My Inhibitions," "Home to My Wandering Appetite," "Ode to a Brown Nude," "Chimera," and "Venado Dreams" first appeared in the essay "Poetry of the Flesh," which appeared in For Colored Boys Who Have Considered Suicide When the Rainbow is Still Not Enough: Coming of Age, Coming Out, and Coming Home (Magnus Books, 2012).

Epigraph: From Loose Woman. Copyright © 1994 by Sandra Cisneros. Published by Vintage Books, a division of Random House, Inc., and originally in hardcover by Alfred A. Knopf, Inc. By permission of Susan Bergholz Literary Services, New York, NY and Lamy, NM. All rights reserved.

Cover Art: Floyd Johnson
Title: I Am a Fruit!
Medium: Oil on Canvas

Author Photo: Fabian Echevarria

Published by Kórima Press
San Francisco, CA
www.korimapress.com

ISBN: 978-0-9889673-5-9

for tatiana de la tierra

Contents

III. BELOW SELENA OR ZAPATA

Foreword

by Ernesto Javier Martínez, Ph.D.

The title of this collection of poetry, *Amorcito Maricón*, cleverly invokes Pedro Infante's iconic interpretation of a song similarly titled ("Amorcito Corazón"). Readers familiar with this allusion—to Golden Age Mexican cinema and, more generally, with the serenata tradition of declaring romantic affection publicly—will find it difficult not to hear the musical reference instantly. They will read the title and most likely experience a kind of transference, or what I would like to call a pause in the illusion of the present, putting the book down to make room for the semblance of collective memory, mouthing lyrics barely remembered, almost one's own, smiling at the end rhyme slippage between "Corazón" and "Maricón." What a wonderful way to begin a collection of poetry dedicated to brown-on-brown joto love—with Infante-esque *ternura* and unabashed joto longing, with song and legacy of romantic ritual. And who better to provoke this palimpsetic encounter than a queer xicano tlacuilo/ tlamatinime, contemporary scribe and shaman, who chronicles *and* interprets the emotional geography of joto love into collective awareness.

Amorcito Maricón is an unashamed and shameless tribute to the cosmology of brown-on-brown desire and love. It is, in every sense, *joto worship*, an eagerly awaited altar (in the guise of irreverent poetry) where readers might come to kneel and find new ways to pray. But what to pray for in a context where new ways of thinking, feeling and knowing have been blessed? In Herrera y Lozano's imaginary, there are certain givens. Rimming another brown man is a spiritual opening. Clubbing is ceremony. Cuming becomes the flight of golondrinas. More than simply trafficking in metaphors, this collection of poetry conjures and communes with our fears and deepest longings, allowing us the opportunity to "pray" in the most embodied and sexually liberating way, honoring each other's bodies and minds with the reverence once only reserved for deities.

Among the stand out qualities of this collection is its insistent cultural embeddedness. There is no universal queerness to be found here, only "children of sarape-covered couches." Queer xicano practices of self-enunciation—i.e., practices of representing oneself, of speaking *with* each other, in culturally specific ways, without preface and apology—are too few in the contemporary literary landscape. In this collection of poetry, however, maricones call each other amorcitos, they invoke gay Latino ancestors lost too soon, demand respect in the ever present context of racist and homophobic hostility, and still make space for sexual pleasure and frivolity, not to mention tongue-in-cheek picardías. How delightful to "pray" at Herrera y Lozano's irreverent altar of joto love and longing. What a beautiful reminder that Herrera y Lozano is, indeed, who we knew him to be in his first collection of poetry: a self-proclaimed, in no need for canonization, Santo de la Pata Alzada.

Ernesto Javier Martínez
November 20, 2013
Eugene, Oregon

GRACIAS. NATÉRARABÁ. THANK YOU.
Acknowledgments

Many hands have touched the poems on these pages. Many hearts have nurtured my own. Many bodies have joined mine. Many minds have played hide-and-seek with me. Many poets have shown me the way.

Acknowledging the countless ones who helped birth, shape, sharpen, and finally release this book, is a difficult task. In part because my memory betrays me. Also, because some names I never learned. So many lives, kin, lovers, those who I betrayed, those who betrayed me, those I long for, those stuck in the crevices of my imagination. Herein, my gratitude:

Orlando, the one man brave and patient enough to love me through the many storms, the many earthquakes of which I have been the epicenter. Thirteen years after the first poem I wrote to you, you continue to be an inexhaustible muse, a brave partner, a kind partner. Te amo, perro feo.

José Manuel Aguilar-Hernández (de Hernández). My brother. Fellow survivor of religious and activist fanaticism. I am grateful we came out of those years and eventually found each other. You are a thought partner and a heart partner. Gracias a ti y a Julián for housing me when I needed to be in Los Angeles, deep in Aztlán, to piece these poems together.

Adelina Anthony. Torito after my own heart. Thank you for pushing me (hard) to finish this damn book, for reminding me that our work is necessary. I grow new hearts just to hold this love for you.

Matthew Barksdale Arthur and Oscar Duarte Martínez. Thank you for making San Francisco home, for making home with us. Your friendship, the late nights, the untold stories, the tears, and the laughter are with me always.

Marisa Becerra. Our Zen Ranchera. You are the standard against which I measure my future self. The serenity in your voice, the fortitude in your mirada, the stillness in your touch, and your love of poetry show my atheist heart that divinity is possible.

Rajasvini Bhansali and Keisha Adams. Thank you for feeding me as I wrote this book. For not dozing off each time I tried describing this project. For having my back when I was scared to keep writing.

Ahimsa Timoteo Bodhrán. The innumerable hours spent on the phone, long before we met in person, tracing identity, struggle, history, shared and distant kin, men, poetry, and winters, helped these poems make sense.

Sharon Bridgforth. My Reverend. My Mentor. My Guide. My Grounding Force. I have been a faithful and grateful follower of your teachings since the night we met in Austin in 2001. I'm still learning.

Tom Capuchin. You brought me back from more ledges than I wish to remember. I cherish your patience, your scolding, your ability to hold me at my anxiety-ridden worst.

T. Jackie Cuevas and Jennifer Margulies. How do I thank the people who made my biggest dream possible? Being published by you, by Evelyn Street Press, by a feminist press, gave me the courage that has carried me to this point. You made me a published writer and shaped me along the way. Oh, thank you. Thank you.

Dino Foxx. My girl, gurl, gurk, and hurl. You are so special to my heart that even my fingers, in their subconscious texting typos, are still trying to define how sacred you are to me. You are my poet spirit.

Francisco J. Galarte. My brother Frank, I am so grateful that our paths have crossed, that queer stars aligned and conspired in our favor. Your words, your work, show me that I have much to learn and grow, that a fuller human me is on its way.

Armando García. Mi Rancherito Chido, gracias por el apoyo que me brindaste aún sin conocerme, por la fe que tuviste en mí y en mis poemas. Gracias, carnal.

Eric-Christopher García. The words you used to describe my work at the 2013 NACCS panel on Joto Poetry reinvigorated the hunger to claim my identity as a joto poet, to not relent. You are a comadre por vida.

Rigoberto González. You believed in this book before I finished explaining it to you. You had faith in this little joto before you even read my first book, later writing my first review. You are the mentor I aspire to be.

Priscilla A. Hale. Big Bill, Sir, thank you for continuing to believe in me, in my poetry, for creating the opportunity for me to return to *allgo* as an artist in residence, for taking me back to Resistencia, where it all began.

Michael Hames-García. My spirit animal. There has not been a minute by your side that I have not cherished. Your heart, your mind, your hands have taught me new ways of knowing and being in freedom.

Ernesto Javier Martínez. Hermoso. You are the truest reminder that brown men like us can and must be present, fierce, patient, and clear. To have your genius and heart open this book with its foreword is an honor I hope future generations know I enshrined for the rest of my days.

Floyd Johnson. My fellow Chihuahuense. For over a decade, your paintings have inspired and excited me. The vision and craft imbedded in every one of your strokes are poetry on the canvas and on the page. Thank you for allowing your art to be on the cover of this book.

Cherríe L. Moraga. Maestra, thank you for making people like me possible. I have been learning from you from afar since my errant youth, never did I imagine that one day I would learn from you up close. Thank you for teaching me to let go, to recognize that once released, this work is no longer mine, sino de nuestra gente.

Emma Pérez. My butch mentor. From the first time we shared a cab in Chicago and I dedicated a reading of "Making Chicano History" to you I have carried this mad joto crush and aspiration to hold an ounce of your brilliance and swagger.

Martha Ramos-Duffer. Where would I be without the countless hours spent trying to make sense of the world we live in, so we could imagine the world we believe possible. So much of you, of us, lives in these poems.

Verónica Reyes. The feedback you gave this manuscript when it was in its earliest form was invaluable in challenging me to let go of my ways and let the poems take on forms I feared. Those forms are now in this book.

Richard T. Rodríguez. My queer in lak'ech, taking what is sacred and holding it up to the sun. Your critical lens has informed and challenged my understanding of what Ch/Xicanidades we have made indisputably sacred, and how dangerous blind reverence can be. I am an indebted fan.

Anita Tijerina Revilla. Nuestra Mujer Fiera. Thank you for forging a world where love is not only socially constructed, but for insisting that it can and must be constructed in humane, caring, radical, affirming ways.

Marvin K. White. You have shown me that language is not a thing to hide from or behind, but to dive into, unwrap, and curiously and furiously stir to surface what hides beneath the stagnant stench of rules and their limitations. Thank you for making Black and Chicano history with me.

Emanuel Xavier. My nefarious friend, thank you for paving this road, for letting me walk it with you, for holding the secrets trapped within leather bars, for helping me piece my memories together.

Macondo. Thank you, comunidad, for holding my artist heart all these years. I am profoundly grateful to my fellow writers and to my patient and insightful teachers— Sandra Cisneros, Ruth Behar, Richard Blanco, Joy Harjo, and Kristin Naca.

And, of course, the authors of Kórima Press. What can this dreamer say but thank you, gracias, natérarabá. Thank you, Adelina Anthony, Cathy Arellano, Anel Flores, Joseph Delgado, Dino Foxx, Pablo Miguel Martínez, Maya Chinchilla, Claudia Rodriguez, Joe Jiménez, Pepe Aguilar-Hernández, Jesús Alonzo, Jackie Cuevas, Rita Urquijo-Ruiz, and Candace López for trusting me, for being patient with me, for inspiring me. This journey feels worthy because of you.

Amorcito
Maricón

"Say my name. Say it.
The way it's supposed to be said."

Sandra Cisneros
"Dulzura"
Loose Woman

I. SARAPE-COVERED COUCHES

DADDY'S BOY
after Reinaldo Arenas

I am that daddy's boy with the round, firm panza,
whose coy smile gropes and fondles your mind,
wraps it in Star Wars sheets.
I am that daddy's boy with the clumsy, chubby hands
tugging at the skirt of your fantasies.
A baby dyke cooing in the playground of church lady laps.
I tug, gnaw, muerdo
on the chicharrón of your inhibitions.

I am that stubborn daddy's boy
running through the candy shop aisles of your legs,
finding the paleta at the end of my travieso jog.
I am that boy playing under the one working street lamp;
tus canicas en mi mano.

I play hide-n-seek with your eyelashes
in front of the Conasupo, where tired men
drank the sun out of their bodies.
I drink the fear out of yours.

I am that screaming daddy's boy, never slackening,
who kicks your pew from behind during misa.
This is my warning:
> If angry you turn and scold me
> I will jump and lick the body of Christ from your mouth.

I am that asthmatic child who smiles,
before cousins and public schools taught him to frown.
A Kool-Aid-framed grin to remind you:
> This is what playground laughter felt like.

I am that spoiled daddy's boy
pouting away your resistance.
You are my Ken doll.
I am your G.I. Joe.

CHILDREN OF WILTED SUNS

At the dawn of becoming a man
tests dressed me in the red
thorny laced gown that once
wrapped the necks of men,
men who loved as I love.

Children of sarape   covered   couches
       of atole   raised   abuelas
      of velvet   Jesus   churches;
                  died   alone
                died in   shame
     in pale   green   hospitals.

Children owed another day
waiting long, waiting still
for golondrinas to   paint their sky.

At the dawn of becoming a man
I donned drapes of their destiny.
I became home
          home to   men
who   love as I   love.

I am home.
Home to men who broke as I break.
Men who wait. Wait in me
for the   flight of   golondrinas.

I am the   couch   to their sarape.
They are the   atole   that raises me,
the velvet   Jesus   hanging over my bed.

I am the   orphan   to their souls,
carrier of   pillaged   dreams.
The son of   men   who died for love.
Love   airbrushed   on the walls inside
                me.

Spirits   dance   every time
I kiss a man   in offered   sacrifice.
Sacrifice to the memory   of wilted suns.

I am home
      home to   men
who kissed as I   kiss.

MONSTERS UNDER OUR BEDS

You inspire a lip-synched
Tiffany song from a joto boy.
El niño sale, comes out to
comb Barbie's hair with you.

You remind me of Sunday morning
cartoons in underwear,
El niño quiere, whispers
Color Purple lines through Duvalín breath.

I would steal roses from 'Macitas flower bed for you;
cry, lie, throw a K-Mart tantrum,
pout until you come out to play.

Have that denied birthday party.
Give you my Chuck E Cheese's ears.
Let you blow the candles on my cake.
Give you all my tokens.
Let you play with my presents
before they're exchanged for
husky Buggle Boy jeans.

You inspire sleepovers:
            sabana-made tents and flashlights.
            Tricycle rides on hot summer days.

Two boys laughing
that Nick-at-Nite laugh,
tickling the tip of my hair.

Come. Play under the fading light post.
Find me first during hide-n-seek.
Hold my hand in the dark,
I'll never tell.

Help me find purpose in
watching sports when I could be
playing house with you instead.

Remind me why children smile
for no reason at all,
before they learn what sin is.

Hold my hand, maybe,
in the playground of haunting
monsters under our beds.

JOTOS

jotos   build   movements   in each other's arms
recite   manifestos   with barely a sound
create   ceremony   on dancefloors
we are the   dead   angels   under each other's feet

jotos   kiss   bruised   after school bullies
find   beauty   in thick, thin, absent hair
our calves   carry   drumbeats,   we are echoes
kept as   walnuts'   shells   guarding their souls

virgins,   mighty,   soft,   callous
unwrapped,   re-birthed,   penetrated,   full
wounded   hands   and still   we feed

jotos   rejoice   in unsubtle   feathers and sparkle
dance under   suns   hovering   above dance floors,
above   we are   bright,   we are woven
spirits,   almost
free

CHIMERA

"Something that exists only in the imagination and is not possible in reality."

— Merriam-Webster

And because I straddle
I am desert-risen culebra,
I am McDonald's-fed Nintendo player,
concrete stuck under the fingernails of memory.
I am the hole in a teenager's old shoe,
his first public erection.

I eat dirt from adobe walls,
drink hope from strangers' mouths.
There is no logic to follow me,
only shriveled reveries.
And yet I straddle.

I am medley of unanswered plegaria.
A novena for AIDS-related deaths,
novena for my own.
For the generation that shares my bed,
I recite *Hail Papi*. For us.

I am my greatest danger:
        a lover of many lovers.
Chuparrosa in a sea of bougainvilleas,
abeja de seis panales.
I am altar to nameless sugar skulls,
a concoction of mismatched dreams.

Until you kiss me
making sense of my fabrications.
I become theory, stuck on your tongue.
I become tongue, stuck on conclusions.

HERRERA Y LOZANO

And because I straddle
1 am decay of alamedas,
the haunting of low-rider days.
A rebel creeping through no-cruise zones.

I loiter, beg
for memories of those who could not leave.
My soul is the echo of canyon walls.

I am becoming another's beautiful:
          gray, thick, and carved by the knife of time.
I am the mirror of men I have chased—
older, not wiser, only older.

Of the lines carved out by time,
I guard them all. All
are love, and pain, and loss,
are greedy children
missing teeth, drooling in bed.
I obey their tantrums, concede,
offer them candy from other lips,
flavored lube, condoms that feel nonexistent,
absent as the one bent before me.

I break bread with so few
make bread of so many.
I expand inside them,
they are PCP to my dilated eyes.

They cum, I go.
As stone-butch dykes do.
Though not as masculine,
often, as untouched.

HOME TO MY WANDERING APPETITE

The faultline of your mountain range
draws my mouth as morning pulls the sun.
As the moon tugs the sea
       my tongue a ravage wave,
       beating you with every dive.

The Southside of your bustling back
becomes home to my wandering appetite.
Every homeless sigh hides from the cold in you.
Every fingertip wanders the back alleys of your neck.

The steep descent my breath makes into you
threatens to leave me trapped
in the moist grasp of your forested mountain walls,
the sweet divide of flavor and gratitude.

I dive, I climb, I grasp
until the wild white doves of
your church tower take flight.
I fall. I rest. I know. I am.

COLONIZED

You might be the one to conquer this empire,
the tall one who perplexed me,
the one I thought was godsent.

You are the heroin Reagan fed to barrio boys.
Awakening the cholo asleep inside me,
my razorblade is sharpened,
isn't for shaving.

If only eating you wasn't toxic,
if you weren't fast food dipped in poison,
I would have never craved you.

You are an Esta Noche dream,
you are the contest.
You are the crown I parade to make them jealous.
Untill your Cortez comes to take it—
he beat me, he won you.

You are my own Duke of Earl.
Victory Outreach banging at my door.
The hydraulics in my chest.
Spinning rims I can't afford.
And I ride you
slowly.

INVOCATION

Be my Virgen.
Be the goddess,
to decorate the room with roses,
shower you with wine and grapes—
make you my aparition.

Be my landfill.
Be my playground,
to rumige through trash bags of feelings,
looking for broken toys from broken boys—
let me fix them.

Be my corruption.
Be my politician,
mi Salinas de Gortari.
Run away with all I give you,
cause my tortilla price to reach the sky.
Make me your broke(n) México of the 90s.

Be my addiction.
Be my Bohemia,
imported beer brewed to my liking.
I'll be your yuppy vodka served with olives,
on the rocks, not shaken.
Chug, don't sip me.

PIEDRA DEL CAMINO

"Dirás que no me quisiste."

— José Alfredo Jiménez

Ken had Barbie
Jesus his prophets
Obama has his "hope"
I have empty pockets.
I tried to do the math
and fell off track.

The moon has its waves
C.I.A. its excuses
Christians have their wait
Catholics redundant traditions
I have warrants and asthma.

And you don't seem to care
for them, for us
for the *Inconvenient Truth.*
You wanted more.

You offered me a bite—
I stayed to feast.
Offered up a rhyme—
a book was born.
Tugged slightly at my heart—
I made love of a crush.

Hummed a Michael Jackson oldie—
I began to dream.
You'd be my Lisa Marie,
a Neverland kind of love.

I dug my own grave on your bedroom floor,
stayed beneath piles of dirty clothes.
I made tepache of your juice:
        bitter, acid, strong.
Spiked with my fate, I was drunk.

I meant to be a one-time song,
became an extended medley.
Rhythm-less and awkward
stuck in your throat like frat boy tequila.
Useless, vile, and crass
like a Tea Party winner.

I loved out of place
betrayed colonial commandments.
Lusted over my neighbor's man.
Lusted, loved, and fucked him.
I'm stubborn as a flu:
        clingy, gross, and viral.

And you didn't seem to care.
Behind closed doors
you were El Rey.
Yo, una piedra en tu camino.

STING

Old Spice burning a fresh shave, the sting.
Your tongue dug deep and broke;
you are in me now.

As an onion bite you bring me to tears.
No one stops the craving;
I bite harder.

You are a Texas flood
unearthing my buried bodies.
Gutters dragging limbs into the river,
off to fertilize down the hill.

Few dared swim the sewage in me.
Until you. Swimming deep.
You took the plunge, barely survived.

The sand I build my love on continues to shift.
Growing creeks slash in a swift grip.
I start over.

Perversely oblique as back seats of a car: this is love.
Hidden in the crevices of stitches and tears;
hiding among French fries and loose change.

In a Superwoman twirl
footsteps carved out our destiny.
I am not alone.
I have the sting.

PAPEL PICADO

I have grown accustomed to your scent.
Perhaps I will miss you.
Tomorrow I will mention this day,
perhaps to lament.

Tomorrow, I might reminisce
beating the piñata of a memory,
knowing no candies remain.

I bit too much of this cake.
I bit too much of you.
Now that my heart starts to ache
I crave a bite.

I am too strong to beg.
You, too fearful to surrender.
Damned by the men we loved.
Damned by the men we have become.

As roosters' crow, we were ecstasy.
Coyotes of a full moon.
Papel picado wrapped around this dream
tore with a tug.
Ripping, cutting into me.

I grew accustomed to your scent.
Perhaps I will smell you
in the necks of strangers who will not hold me
in our afterglow.

Perhaps I will conjure you once.
Mariachi, my song at your window.
Romantically stalking your movement,
too fearful to strike.
Perhaps you will miss me one day.
I will never know.

SOBER

We were once salvaged lust.
Hungry thralls, hopeless thralls.
We were once reckless fun.
You were salt, I was wound.

We were violent—
old and childish,
grasping for youth,
grasping for ourselves.

The beds we shared we detested,
drowned them in vodka, in olives.
I played a song of regret.
You smirked, you hummed it.

Our tongues dripped lime.
Our arms wove cumbias.
You were medicine and side effect.
Though you were trite, you never defected.
I swallowed all: your cum, your spite.

We were saints.
We were virgins.
Loved on weekends,
in times of need.

Hungover on lust I grew nauseous.
Ate you as a cure to my infection.
Welcomed our lies. I wrote myths.
Not you. You hid them.

We were tepache, more bitter than sweet.
We drank ashes from urns.
Ashes of men we regret.
Olives we pitted,
limes we squeezed to death.

I vomited our world and defected.
Stumbling through cans of Tecate,
still craving your salt, tus limones.
Not now.
Now I am sober.

YOU BRING OUT THE JOTO IN ME

after Sandra Cisneros

You bring out the Joto in me.
The María Felix eyebrows.
The sexually confused macho.
The Tecate & lime.
The Saturday morning shock
of hickies and phone numbers.
You are the one I would hold hands
in public with, while cruising down my old barrio.
Allow you other men in bed, still believing
promises of monogamy and forever.
Definitely. Definitely.
For us.

You bring out the Chelo Silva in me.
The bolero in me.
La mano caída, tight jeans, and spiked hair in me.
The velvet dress on a Sunday morning,
unshaved legs with white nylons in me.
The spine of Frida in me.
The butchered Coyoxauqui in me.
The screaming super market baby in me.
The government cheese in me.
The chismoso y metiche in me.
The fetish of crucifixes on hairy chests in me.
The J pronounced as Y in me.
The greasy, mullet-like wavy hair in me.
The Chihuahua desert, pecans, and red meat in me.
The love of death in me.
You know you do.
Oh, you know you do.

You bring out the drag queen in me.
The perpetual attitude in me.
The Juan Gabriel trip and fall in me.
The Rivera-inspired Catrina in me.
The gay bar bathroom bump in me.
The *Bidi-Bidi-Bom-Bom* in me.
The San Antonio 3:00 a.m. fideo con carne in me.
The fondling on the dance floor in me.

Papacito. My sweet obsession.
I am the psycho who stalks your home at night,
make sure you're there when you say so.
I would find a man just to cheat on him with you.
I want to bottom, top, flip it, and reverse it with you.
I want to commit unforgivable sins and bask in them.
I want to trade Grey Goose for Boones Farm,
coke for crack, Banana Republic for the Gap.
Me sacas lo maricón en mí,
y te gusta, chulo.

You bring out the ojo-giving celoso in me.
The "I'm gonna cut her if he don't stop starin' at you" in me.
The high-heel-stabbing Esta Noche diva in me.

The blank-stares at football games in me.
The Texas syphilis breakout in me.
The AIDS pandemic in me.
The Out Magazine never seen Mexican cover-boy in me.
I'd mispronounce my name for you,
light a cigarette and watch how others lust for you;
ready to burn whoever gets too close.

Sabes que soy cabrón.
Soy San Lorenzo quien quema los pies dc noche.
I am the excessive drinker.
The insatiable size queen.
The sex-addicted promiscuity.
You bring out the superficial lust at-first-sight in me.
The vile jealousy in me.
The voyeur and exhibitionist in me.
The leather daddy in me.

Sage. Pomada de la Campana. Concha Nacar.
Hierbaloca. Jabón ZOTE. Mota. Sal de Uvas.
Lavender candles.
All you locas, talented and not,
Marisela Monet, Kelly Kline, represent, girls.

I want to be your loca.
Only your papi. Be my papi.
I want to show you the way jotos do it.
The way we were meant to.

II. CABALLERO SALUDOS

FLAME

I am the fire of suns on campesino backs,
eclipsed in the shadow of your ass in my hands.
Dancing venado, sweat down my chest.
Where men come to rest.
Where love comes to die.

BANDIDO OF YOUR AFTERNOONS

I come with the afternoon
kissing away stubborn regrets
crushing guilt with the   drop of your   pants.

Hair of our chests grind Catholic disdain.
Underwear wet with your welcome,   drenched
as caballero saludos are violently exchanged.

I come with no pistols
        your peaceful vaquero.
Though I come with no peace;
I come to make you my lover.

I come in full daylight
parading for all your vecinos   peeking
through humid windows,   imagining
what I come for,   what I take.

I leave with the afternoon.
Saddle fast and gallop into traffic stampedes
smelling   you   on my   fingertips.

As vultures circle the dead
my patience circles each day.
For when you reappear with orders
I saddle, race to verboten land.

EL OTRO

You have the best off all worlds,
enjoy the rollercoaster thrill:
      someone who calls you his man
      another to share your bed.

He might cradle your stories,
I'm the one who appeases
the spirits in your body chanting,
waking the serpent in my nopalera.

Starring in my own telenovela
I ride in when no one is looking.
A cliché galán with a weakness for
the lips of another's hombre.

Perhaps I was raised for this,
catholically afraid of commitment.
So I feast on yours hoping he can't smell
my kisses on your back when he hugs you at night.

I graze on virgin nerves
along neglected curves,
knowing I am cursed for preying on your vices.
But I can't let go, I wont let go.

The potrillo in my body
gallops hard when you ride.
When your legs tighten my hips into place
harnessing this weak heartbeat.

The soldadera roaring in me
highjacks the train of my feelings,
throwing out my inhibitions.
I am for here for your taking.

For a moment you are mine, not his;
when you pick up the pace and claim me.
When the virgin nerves along neglected curves
go deaf in the burst that draws your name on my stomach.

When breath is faint and words are absurd,
coyly, I wait to hear you say
you are mine for the night.
But you cant let go. He wont let go.

AMORCITO MARICÓN
por Manuel Esperón

Amorcito Maricón,
yo tengo tentación
de un beso.

De añadirme al sudor
que emite tu pudor
cuando yo

dejo de ser
otro ser
al estar en ti.

Te quiero ver
otra vez
sollozar.

Lamerte en la región
donde no ilumina el sol,
quisiera.

Amorcito Maricón,
alimenta mi obsesión
por ti.

Enredados una noche más,
no hagas caso
lo que digan los demás.

Amorcito Maricón,
serás mi amor.

SUEÑOS HIERÁTICOS
para Pepe y Julián

Soñé un amor revolucionario, prófugo e irreverente,
arraigado en la memoria de tierras soberanas. Un amor que surge,
emana desde los poros de mi infancia: inocente y precoz;
puro a mi manera.

Te soñé a ti. También, descendiente de un pasado de abundancia,
fruto de estampidas ceremoniales. Tus raíces emitiendo un ritual
antiguo, mas no olvidado. Tus dedos acariciando eminentes alegorías,
esperanzas de libertad, de autonomía declarada— no otorgada.

Soñé lo nuestro. Una unión profetizada, hilvanada en la historia
de nuestros pueblos. Forjada por la reyerta de ideales, sueños.
Inexhaustos sueños. Movimientos que nos parieron.

Soñé este encuentro. Como dos planetas resistiendo dictaduras
orbitales, nos encontramos. Aquí, en un mar de incandescentes
batallas, mis sueños se manifiestan en carne, música y un beso hierático.

TORERO

Your thighs— my trigger
spell that is cast
phosphorous that enkindles
calves on the brink of harvest.
Campesino in me awoken
ploughing through this lust
ploughing through us.

Coloring you by numbers.
Tracing your spots.
Lick, taking you as communion.
Wanting to keep a piece of you—
          a scent, a cell, a chant.
Taunting this beast of lust.
Taunting this beast of us.

This lust is a blister.
My hands dig through your gravel
     (pain somewhere in the distance)
seeking Aldebaran in you.
Be torero who found his bull,
waving the red of lust
the red in us.

Skidding across your chest,
pebbles skipping across this lake.
My fingertips, my lips
sunk into your flesh.
Nostalgic as this memory.
Blaspheming the rules of lust.
Blaspheming for us.

FESTEJO

Eres mi trago:
thick, rimmed with salt.
Your neck, los limones, dripping.

Eres molcajate:
mi chile fits your taste.
Coarse from grinding, burning.

Eres mi hambre:
you are my Christmas slay.
Stabbed, running, bleeding.

Yo soy la muerte:
my altar your back,
my fingertips its candles.

THE AGAVE OF MY THIGHS

"I'd like to direct your attention to something that needs directing to."

— Madonna

Lick the smooth and moist
crevice of fingerprints and joy.
Tickle the bitterness away.
Lather me with memory and hope.

Wipe the smirk off my face
with traction of hunger and thirst.
Enough stubble to cause enough pain
to ask for more.

Whispers pidiéndote más:
    Dale, papi, cómeme más.
Take and break this bread,
eat till you walk away
smelling of a mama's boy.

Stab me with the girth,
lengua you use to praise the Lord;
trained by abuela's spices.
Find my taste reminiscent:
        fruta, lime, chile, dulce.

Lick away the curse,
ojo que me diste al llegar.
Rub huevo over your face,
flip remedios on their head.
Set me free.

Tear the agave of my thighs,
open the floodgate.
Come, drink and dance
in the fandango of my body.
Leave drunk, slurring, happy.

AMORCITO MARICÓN

COSECHA

"La tierra es de quien la trabaja con sus manos."

— Emiliano Zapata

Trotando por el campo de tu espalda
tropiezo por el adobe de tu piel erizada.
Canto y bailo entonado por tu llanto,
como manantiales brotando
al atravesar tu serranía.

Rozo la flor de tu acequia.
Mis dedos se deshidratan.
Mi nogal se agita.
Tu noria me guía.

Vagando por tus llanos caigo al río
que ruge creciente por tu bajío.
Me baño en la bulla,
la corriente me lleva,
las rocas me cortan como cuando niño.
Mis surcos secos, ahora anegados
brotan de vida con el fresco de nuestro rocío.

Cosechando lo que sembraste
la semilla atrabancada crece salvaje.
Monto el caballo de tu lirio.
Desentierro, sacudo, disfruto
el fruto recluso de tu tierra brava y morena.
Me pierdo en el laberinto de tus maizales
aruñado y al final encontrando la mazorca.

Barbechando la tierra prieta de tu cabellera,
el olor de tu polvo me carga y arrulla.
Me hace darte, montarte.
Regar con mi cantera tus labios.
Echarle leña a tu hoguera.
Haciéndote mío como lo hiciera mi gente,
expulsando al terrateniente.
Que esta es mi tierra.

CACERÍA

Ay del que se ha de encontrar
atrapado en tu trinchera,
trepado sobre tu espalda
donde me quisiera fincar.

Montarme y permanecer
aferrado como una plaga,
infectándote las ganas
que me pretenden arrancar.

Acechando la ruta
que suele esconder,
la selva misteriosa
donde me quiero perder.

Aruñado por mesquites
al subir tus cerritos.
Cruzando por tus piernas,
susurrarte "Chiquito."

Cantando y chiflando,
pregonando mi fe.
Espantar los coyotes
que te pretenden comer.

Por gula o locura
ningún otro buey
ha de probar los sabores
que apenas cacé.

MEMBRILLO LEAVES IN A STORM

When the dust of our passion settles
When you are taken by fresher gusts
    I will fade as the summer moon
    a slow death making way for another.
    I will fall as cathedrals built on sacred land
    sinking into abysmal, forgotten claws
        leaving kisses as artifacts for you.

You will join the unending list
made of languid covenants, lies, droughts.
As promises sowed
destroyed before harvest
by the hail of your disinterest.

I know this story well.
As winter to the crops, you are fatal.
Arid land that I am, I drink you.
This is not a riddle.

A deluge of tears will whelm me,
purging you of me.
Still, I avoid higher ground away from you.

There is no fleeing your laugh
    puerile and bleakly scattered—
    teasing me as wind to a kite.

My descent will be ruthless.
Tossed and abandoned
as membrillo leaves in a storm.

I know this.
Yet each day, like a flower,
I stretch my frailty wide.
Hoping your boots wont crush me
as you march to other soil.

Leaving would be in vain. I am a coward.
I am desert animal. You are raindrops to my thirst.
And I live off so little.

I am oafish and vassal
to the arrogance you emit.
Crumbs are all you need to lure me.

I expect no love to call my own
nor the fire to keep me from freezing.
Desert nights are as vile as your absence.

So I hide under the stone of our moments
          holding the heat of our friction
                    when you dance in my arms
                    when I dream of staying in yours.

MAÍZ

This love is corn—
unfertile, unpure.
Bitter pesticide
altered its growth.

Leaves wrapped around
are alergen to farming hands.
Corrupted aging seed,
less fertile each spring.

Huitlacoche doesn't want me now,
will not grow.
Rats fled seeking new food—
would rather starve.

Worms began to eat their own,
weather other storms,
wont taste this rotting husk.

Stalks that once fed
snap with each blow.
Russling leaves
more silent each dawn.

Machetes grow their rust,
nothing left to cut.
This love is not good feed,
kernals all but broken off.

WEEPING POEM

This poem weeps as a willow.
Its branches slope with every sigh.
Broken twigs pepper its margins.
Its verses frail. Its roots are cold.

This poem does not sway,
sadness lines its bark.
Its words as leaves, begin to fall
turning gold too soon, dying.
This poem weeps because he is gone.

The stems of its metaphors too brittle.
As bearing catkins, its stanzas loll.
His lips as wind, pollinate with kisses.
When he is gone, words bear no hope.

Along the riverbank of heartbreak songs
this poem leans, ready to fall.
Soon it will drown, become debris.
A life too short to count. He is gone.

MINERO LOVERS

My mind is running barefoot and fast
hearing the rumbling of pain,
trying to warn my heart you are on your way.
Hoping to arrive before
your voice hits the foot of my canyon.

These feelings are hidden high
in the mountains of my fear.
Where mining caves abound,
where greedy men stormed through.
You are late at coming around—
excavations left me empty.

Raw material of faith once lined these walls.
Exploited and dragged away,
no minerals of hope left for you.
Only emptiness and decay,
remains from years of explosives.

Dried ravaged veins of my heart
carried nuggets of golden love, copper lust.
Quenching the thirsty wandering about
these rivers roared emanating from springs of trust;
now they are empty.

Warning signs coat my chest
desperate to keep you out,
keep you from tripping on the twigs—
remnants of failed attempts,
from getting lost in the trails
falling into abandoned wells of the forgotten.

Nothing is left of the rich
full Copper Canyon of my early days.
Only echoes from the vast emptiness left behind,
brutal footprints in the ground from the fleeing
minero lovers who once mined me.

III. BELOW SELENA OR ZAPATA

MAKING CHICANO HISTORY
after Marvin K. White

You make me want to
tattoo another teardrop below my left eye,
re-do my eyebrows with a sharpie,
see how high my bangs can go.

You are
the first wave of braseros
planting seeds across my back.
Yours are the brown raindrops
coating this land,
washing away the toxic ashes of other loves.
My love, turn my land,
make it ours again.

I want to make Chicano history with you.
Be your Miguel Hidalgo
and scream independence
down your throat.
Let you swim across my river defiant.
I want you to reclaim your name in my lips,
want to be your asylum.
Want you to stomp on these borders
till minute men remember they don't belong.
I wanna make some Chicano history with you.

Be the first man to call you his Aztlán.
I want to create new words to describe you.
Roll my tongue three times to evoke you.
Show you how my H is silent,
My R's are heavy.

I wanna make Chicano history with you.
Re-write that cumbia admiring the beauty of your ass
porque *es lindo tu cucu.*
Want to carry you to my homeland,
back to mi tierra.
Show you how I learned what I know
with the stem of an onion.
Want to dance like the devil over desert planes,
make you thirsty just by watching,
quenched by the salt of my tongue.
Carry you back to Texas over my shoulder.
Be the Pipila
guarded from the stones of my past,
come to haunt me one more time.

I wanna make Chicano history with you.
Write your manifesto.
Be the Joaquín of your movimiento.
Have family outings at the nearest rest stop.
Remind me how we're more Black and Indio
than white and Spanish—
denounce that hispanic bullshit.
I want to birth more mestizos with you.
Cook nopales and chacales for you.
Something moist.
Something rough.

See, I wanna make some Chicano history
with you.
Want to run through public classrooms
every 5 de Mayo
and remind folks it's not independence day.

I wanna be your Chávez,
make this world safe for you.
You be the Guadalupe who guides and carries me
when I've been beaten once again.
Be the gentle croon that makes my hips sway.
Before reggaetón y rock en español,
when pretty men galloped away into the sunset.
I wanna gallop my way into you
una vez
otra vez
porque vez
esta vez

I just
wanna make some Chicano history with you.
Want you to cruise back into my barrio
my name sketched around your neck,
airbrushed on the hood of your car
below Selena or Zapata.

I wanna sit in the middle seat of your troca.
Like my mama makin' sure girls knew who was dad's ruca.
Want to give ojo to any cabrón who dares eye you.
Flash the razorblade I hide in my chongo
while twirling my fingers through your sideburns.
'Cuz you are my man
in all those ways I've been taught are unhealthy.
Tell you I'd die without you.
I'd cut anyone trying to get close to you.
Or if my politics overcame me,
I'd at least drill some Catholic guilt into you.
The kind even Jesus can't remove.

The kind that made daddy buy mom more
Jafra
Payless shoes and
Home Interior.

I want my home to be your interior.
I want to be the corn in your maseca.
Glide between your fingers,
stick underneath your nails.
Want to come home with you every Thanksgiving;
eat your mama's stuffing.

Sí, papi.
Build me a house on Mango Street.
Where people look like you and me.
Where no one answers their doors.
Where no one knocks before entering.
Where our children run free.
Where having a papá and a daddy
makes no one blink.

See, I just want to make some Chicano history
with you.
Be the warrant that finally gets you.
And free you.
I'll expunge your three strikes
like that fancy lawyer did for uncle Tony.

We will stand beside the founding mothers
of this country, our country.
Not the red, white and blue
nor the green, white and red.
For both have denied us.
This land, our land, is an ancient land.

I will learn to run through canyons like my ancestors.
Carrying chile pasado and my love.
And I shall feed you.
And I shall continue
makin' some Chicano history
with you.

HIERBALOCA:
THE CHILDREN OF AZTLÁN

May we dance
in the living room of hope.
Our bodies hold memory—
we are desert stones.

May we rise
in the face of our pain.
As Arizona weeds dare,
our fists rise most when blown.

Our hearts pump through sorrow
making way for what is possible.
We are farmers. We harvest our own.

We are backyard children
playing, watched by la abuela
weaving through each other's arms.

We are leaves
on branches, on roads.
Fodder after being shade
          cover to elders
food for new leaves to grow.

We are blood
rivers, mama's veins.
We are the return,
though we never left.

Our lungs pump through anguish
manifest what is possible.
We are Texas breeze in each other's hair.

We are nopal-raised abuelos
we play dice with tomorrow
betting: we will overcome.

Somos, todos, aztlaneros.
Our roots run deep, run wild.
Unharnessed, tainted as the Gulf.

We were free. We remember.
Thievery shall not hold us.
We have no papers to show.

ODE TO A BROWN NUDE
after Pablo Neruda

With   jagged
              breathing.
With   hunger racing
                    to reach your body.
Grasping a   thread of light.

So I may carve you onto the walls of my memory:
      Lying naked in the afternoon
      hidden from the hands of a Texas sun.
      Shipwrecked off the sea of my thighs.

Beautifully crude.
As hungry and brown as the Mexican gulf.
Bathed in the black hair of your   mestizaje.
Your   chest,
           stomach,
               legs, all
                    bountiful and
                          wild.

Your lips leave tears along my   s h a f t with each   touch.
With each groan you bring me   closer
to the gods our bodies were meant to worship;
before we were taken,
              stripped   from
                     and made into
    children of a land we   never   left.

The bay of your back holds spirits of other men,
men who   swam   through your coast.
I want to drown among them.
Hike into the mountains of your ass   suffocate
in the dense wilderness of your taste.

In the panting of my thrust
     the stroking of your kisses
     the tattooed bites along your back
          this son of brown gods
                    returns joyful,
                    scarred and free
                    to the valleys of his people.

NATIVE FRUIT

Today I found you
perched as an eagle straddling my legs,
devouring my serpent.
Surrounded by the lake of your bed,
staring back at me with a prophetic gaze.

Years of nomadic fate
choked as your claw tightened further.
I built an empire on this lake
if only for a moment.

Your throat erased political divisions
territories became regions.
You had no beginning,
I had no end.

As Aztlán returning to its whole and holy state
these bodies of men merged.
You fed off my native fruit,
I fulfilled my purpose
if only for a moment.

HERRERA Y LOZANO

CHAC-MOOL

This is where I come to be still
as if fearing the cut of barbwire.
Frozen, stuck between your legs
wrapped in your dulzura.

Crushed by each muscle
tight and making way.
A thunderstorm
waiting to soak and strike.

As a poem filled with my past
you are filled with me;
filled with my present.

Eres como mi tierra
cracked open with heat.
And you swallow me like a raindrop,
a tender seed.

This is where I come to be still
waiting for a gesture to invite me.
Abrirte, plow your fertile soil.
Abriendo brecha en tu dulzura,
burning in the excavation of your body.
Mining for precious stones in each susurro.

As silence torn by a rising dusk
your body speaks to me in forgotten tongues.
My hips obey your every sound.
My stillness
            a breath of air.

My silence is a morning prayer.
Your answer
        the voice of god.

This is where I come to be still
before you come to equal absence.
Before I land at the foot of your temple.

I am sacrifice offered
to the god of your satisfaction.
My heart still beating
in the grip of your hand.

VENADO DREAMS

Last night I dreamt of your besos.
I dreamt of the impious creed– your tongue in me,
your moans calling ancestros.
Drumbeats of ancient days
flickered in heartbeats.

    Vastness of your violent sea
        slashing, making waves in me
                finding home in me
    atado a tus besos.

Tambora,
        your hips,
                your sway
      offered in sacrifice.
This son of Reileras came home.
No rifle left to guard.

I dug, found water in your besos.
The legs of my memories
leaped through mesquite dreams,
brought you sotol to feast.
Feeding you from my hands, uncolonized.
My freedom: your besos.

Licking the treaty scars
        your lips,
                your sighs,
      your stubble and mine.
Re-virgined lands, not occupied.
Libre en tus besos.

Child of revolutions passed,
made your tongue my mast;
flew the flag of this reclaimed man.
No rifle left to guard.

DANZANTES

You plow this land, turn my soil.
Extract my lust for you. For us.
You make me home.
You are my drink at last call
the phone number I smile to at dawn
the backside I claw

the temple stairs I toss my beating heart down.
You eat my pulse, parade it around.
My feathered serpent guard.

You are the song I can't zone out.
Make me want to belong, rebel, at once.
I am dancing dear
           prancing through hailing arrows
                       bucking horns in other meadows.

Your pasture is home.
You let me make home with you
           find lust in others eating my fruit
           are both sun, my leaves grow to you
           and earth, my roots drink from you.
You are unruly land.

We are an extended song.
Our dance floor is rough.
Our beat is not smooth.

ÁGUILA Y SERPIENTE

In a lake of neon lights
serpent child of the night
slithered into my eyes.

I found gold
tongue dug deep
mined for peace
in the provincia between your legs.

I found leaves.
I found stones.
Hieroglyphs from other men,
beneath where Popo and Ixta met.

My lips crawled new depths.
Newfangled scent led me there.
This shall be the sacred lake.
I am eagle. You are snake.

Claws opened you wide
flew in for the bite,
acquiesced to your grasp.

I am no more.
Once was free.
Wander the skies,
your scent above my beak.

ANNIVERSARY

Sunlight stabbed my eyes at six.
You are snoring on.
Flowers will be bought at dusk,
reservations once I'm gone.

You'll celebrate the love you have.
Four years dragging along.
He will hold your back tonight,
I'll be in Eastern Aztlán.

Holding tight throughout the night
fending off the ghosts who prey.
Esta noche serás para él.
Treaty reads you're mine till then.

Your breath makes home,
nestles along my neck.
Your fingertips along my thigh.
Stubborn dawn will not relent,
it wants our day.

Tonight I sleep in other arms,
you'll try to hide the mark I left.
He'll fend off my ghosts tonight,
you'll fuck your night away.

Nothing breaks between you and me.
No nuissance of the every day.
No promises that we'll regret.
It's just today.

VESTIGES

All I have to offer is an empty bed,
a stutter to greet you with—
proof that I'm afraid.

The scars along my arms
to coat this confessed pain.
Naïve enough to hold on
hoping you offer a cure.

You lift me from the dew,
a misty-eyed lament.
Pulled me from the one who hurts,
as if hiding me in your den.

Fearful to unwrap this gift.
Afraid to jump, to jump too soon.
I lose myself; fall into you.

Lost in your naked eyes, I obey: undress.
I silence the broken past— gifts of broken men.
I leave them all outside,
leaving them to watch from there.

I begin to mine your neck
traverse your beard to find your lips.
I let my fingers do the walking
let them rest below your back.

I open myself to you.
Feel your mouth harvest this want.
My fingers do the dancing
pulling, prancing through your hair.

You climb my chest to offer a kiss
feeding me a taste of you,
a taste of myself.

Fueled by nomadic pain
I excavate poetic fodder,
offer your moon my snake.

I unbury vestiges of lust.
Emerge from the mine
and find a brighter sun.

I set out to heal you
came out healed by you.
I found myself
by finding you.

TEJANO
after Madonna

I want to kiss you in Austin.
I want to hold your hand in San Antonio.
I want to run naked through El Paso,
make love on a bus to Laredo.
Put you in me.
You know why? This is why.

Claim me, take me, show me
the way tejanos claim their lust.
Chain me, scrape me
the way tejanos own their lust.

I want you to show me
what it's like
to make love in the tongue of your father.
To cut through like the Río Grande river.
To gallop over the memory of other lovers.
Let me see you try to contain me.
Tame me with a bite, brand me.

Show me, guide me, drag me
to where tejanos breed their lust.
Lead me, hold me
to where tejanos take their lust.

Put me in the mood
under the desert moon.
Take me.

Show me what could have been
had the Alamo remained ours.
Would you say my name right?
Would you dare

rewrite the story
perched where men have found god.
Take a ride.

Sow me like the land
your ancestors worked and died on.
Find me, feel me, tell me
how tejanos fall in love.

JESUS IS BLOND

Jesús went blond.
Gave up the ghost on me.
Peroxide turned to a faux gold
hair brown as the Texas sea.

Jesus is gone.
De-chicanofied, he fled.
Defending a lying flag
that wont give a damn.

Now that he's gone
the sky turned blind
by the stars and the stripes,
looking for peace
through the blood of the unfree.

Jesus is lost.
Mapquest wont find his way.
His soul has gone so far away.
Ran off the day blood was shed
for him, for green gods.

Jesus is fraught.
Wandering the aisles of his sin.
Trading off college debt
for children's lives.

Jesus the blond.
Crucified on an oil cross.
Rifle in hand
gave up his life
for the falsely free
for republican dreams.

Jesus is dead.
His body shipped back.
Wrapped in his flag.
Disguised for family to believe
he died for a good deed.

GOLONDRINA:
PLEGARIA FOR GWEN ARAUJO
Transgender Day of Remembrance,
November 20, 2009, Austin, TX

Precious bud
cut as it bloomed.
Precious vessel of possibility
I am lost without you.

        May this night burn in your fire,
           sissy men will be your choir.
        You shall reign the sky.

Heartbeatless ascension
no one can cut your wings.
Golondrina, llévame.

Virgen de Esperanza.
Prophet, our promised child.
RISE!

        May this night burn in your fire,
           sobbing butches bring you flowers.
        You shall reign the sky.

Precious sight: the sight of you.
Hair cascading your shoulders,
breast cupping our truths.

        Esta noche serás reina.
        Serás la flama que nos lleva.
        Golondrina, llévanos.

Stricken by silence,
we are each other's wounds.
We come. We conjure you.

My body. Your altar.
Your spirit is our flame.
RISE!

Swallow beak,
dark and strong.
Carry us to freedom.
Carry us in your wind.

                                        Somos leña en tu hoguera
                                        hijas de tu libertad.
                                        Miel de nuestro paladar
                                        esta noche reinas brava,
                                        el encendio en nuestro cielo.

May this night burn in your fire
queerful children take us higher.   Somos leña en tu hoguera:
You shall reign the sky   Hijas de tu libertad.
Colored star in the night   Miel de nuestro paladar.
live on in our breath.   Esta noche reinas brava
We sing your name.   el encendio en nuestro cielo.

Precious bud cut too soon.
Precious vessel of possibility,
we are found in you.

HONEY CHILD
para Ana Sisnett

Birthed as honey dripping down a mango tree.
Splashing lullabies humming from the sea.
Proclaiming from the earth a sacred being.
Panamá birthed its soul.

Vast, untamed as a morning dawn.
Heart beating out a holy song.
Moving among us as evening fog.
Panamá gave us its own.

My air follows your cadence diffused.
This poet flows finding its muse in you.
Licking love drops as you swim on by.
Hija de Panamá, te sigo yo.

I've grown fins to swim with you.
Learned rhythms to sway my hips like you.
Sought the world through your negra eyes.
Written of our truths.
Grew a Panamenio soul.

GOD IS BROWN

Brown is the color of my god's skin.
Gentle, curvy, older than a Spanish whip.
My god abides outside of sin,
no water needed to baptize the newly born.
Brown is the color of my lover's back.

The color of wombs, tender and soft.
Color of mothers, color of their sons.
Supple and round, violently quiet.
Color of ancestros calling us home.
The color of home.

Brown is the desert of my child's face,
color of woman nestled in her woman's love.
Brown is the only color I know,
dirt from which I grow.

Color once bought, traded as gold.
Color of heaven, color of pride.
Loved by the sun, abandoned by flags.
Transcendent of seasons, the walls of our souls.
The color of hope.

Color of feathers coating my serpent of night.
Hidden from the world, in my stubborn graying curls,
in the Oreo-flavored lips of a lover.

The color of god, the bowl of Chac-Mool.
Legs of a musician strumming my sighs.
Celestial as stars, mundane as a smile.
Holding more meaning than X holds in sounds.

The color of love traced on a man's thigh.
The one who is seeking, the one who is found.
Color de libertad, of borderless bodies,
of borderless writers, of borderless hope.
The color of us.

BIO

A Queer Xicano writer of Rarámuri descent, Lorenzo Herrera y Lozano is the author of *Santo de la Pata Alzada: Poems from the Queer/Xicano/Positive Pen* (Evelyn Street Press).

Along with Adelina Anthony and Dino Foxx, Lorenzo is a co-author of *Tragic Bitches: An Experiment in Queer Xicana & Xicano Performance Poetry* (Kórima Press), and the editor of *Queer Codex: Chile Love* (*allgo*/Evelyn Street Press), and, *Queer Codex: Rooted* (*allgo*/Evelyn Street Press).

A member of the Macondo Writers community, his work appears in *Mariposas: A Modern Anthology of Queer Latino Poetry* (Floricanto Press); *For Colored Boys Who Have Considered Suicide When the Rainbow is Still Not Enough: Coming of Age, Coming Out, and Coming Home* (Magnus Books); *Queer in Aztlán: Chicano Male Recollections of Consciousness and Coming Out* (Cognella); as well as the journals, *ZYZZYVA: the journal of West Coast writers and artists*; and, *Yellow Medicine Review: A Journal of Indigenous Literature, Art, and Thought*. Lorenzo is the editor of the forthcoming *Joto: An Anthology of Queer Xicano & Chicano Poetry*. Lorenzo is the founder of Kórima Press.

Made in the USA
San Bernardino, CA
20 April 2014